Management Systems for Sustainability

How to Connect Strategy and Action

Phil Cumming
Email: **phil.cumming@korusustainability.net**

First published in 2013 by Dō Sustainability
87 Lonsdale Road, Oxford OX2 7ET, UK

ISBN 978-1-909293-82-3 (eBook-ePub)
ISBN 978-1-909293-83-0 (eBook-PDF)
ISBN 978-1-909293-81-6 (Paperback)

A catalogue record for this title is available from the British Library.

Dō Sustainability strives for net positive social and environmental impact. See our sustainability policy at **www.dosustainability.com**.

Page design and typesetting by Alison Rayner
Cover by Becky Chilcott

For further information on Dō Sustainability, visit our website:
www.dosustainability.com

DōShorts

Dō Sustainability is the publisher of **DōShorts:** short, high-value ebooks that distil sustainability best practice and business insights for busy, results-driven professionals. Each DōShort can be read in 90 minutes.

New and forthcoming DōShorts – stay up to date

We publish 3 to 5 new DōShorts each month. The best way to keep up to date? Sign up to our short, monthly newsletter. Go to **www.dosustainability.com/newsletter** to sign up to the Dō Newsletter. Some of our latest and forthcoming titles include:

- ***Sustainable Energy Options for Business*** Philip Wolfe
- ***Adapting to Climate Change: 2.0 Enterprise Risk Management*** Mark Trexler & Laura Kosloff
- ***How to Engage Youth to Drive Corporate Responsbility: Roles and Interventions*** Nicolò Wojewoda
- ***The Short Guide to Sustainable Investing*** Cary Krosinsky
- ***Strategic Sustainability: Why it Matters to Your Business and How to Make it Happen*** Alexandra McKay
- ***Sustainability Decoded: How to Unlock Profit Through the Value Chain*** Laura Musikanski
- ***Working Collaboratively: A Practical Guide to Achieving More*** Penny Walker
- ***Understanding G4: The Concise Guide to Next Generation Sustainability Reporting*** Elaine Cohen
- ***Leading Sustainable Innovation*** Nick Coad & Paul Pritchard
- ***Leadership for Sustainability and Change*** Cynthia Scott & Tammy Esteves

- ***The Social Licence to Operate: Your Management Framework for Complex Times*** Leeora Black
- ***Building a Sustainable Supply Chain*** Gareth Kane

Subscriptions

In addition to individual sales of our ebooks, we now offer subscriptions. Access 60+ ebooks for the price of 5 with a personal subscription to our full e-library. Institutional subscriptions are also available for your staff or students. Visit **www.dosustainability.com/books/subscriptions** or email **veruschka@dosustainability.com**

Write for us, or suggest a DōShort

Please visit **www.dosustainability.com** for our full publishing programme. If you don't find what you need, write for us! Or suggest a DōShort on our website. We look forward to hearing from you.

Abstract

ALL BUSINESSES SMALL OR LARGE will have some form of a management system even if they do not think of it in these terms. It is not necessarily something you see – it is part of the very fabric of a business and what makes it tick. Adopting a management systems approach to tap into and supplement these existing management and governance arrangements can play a crucial part in helping to implement more sustainable ways of working. It will help you in being more formalised and systematic in how and when you do things. It will help people understand what sustainability means and more importantly how it applies to their organisation or role. It will strengthen the link between strategy and action and provide the framework for various things to happen. This DōShort is intended to introduce you to management systems thinking and concepts and sets out clear and practical steps and guidance you can follow to put you in a good position to plan and deliver on your sustainability ambitions – without needing to follow a single management system standard!

About the Author

PHIL CUMMING is an accomplished corporate sustainability manager and consultant with over 15 years' multi-sector experience, which includes developing and managing the delivery of the award-winning sustainability strategy for the London 2012 Games from the ground up; from inception through to its dissolution culminating in the associated learning legacy programme (the first time that a major UK project has attempted to capture intellectual capital on this scale). Prior to London 2012, Phil spent nearly 10 years working in the environmental consultancy sector. After a brief spell at Schumacher College in 2001, he developed a keen interest in finding more sustainable business solutions. A Chartered Environmentalist, a Chartered Waste Manager and an IEMA Registered Environmental Auditor, as a consultant he provided the complete delivery of a range of projects within the sustainability field including due diligence, compliance appraisals, integrated management systems, auditing, waste and resource management and sustainability appraisals, across a diverse number of industrial sectors (such as government, defence, construction, chemical, ICT, food and beverage, transportation and manufacturing) for major private and public sector organisations in the UK and overseas. He was Head of the UK Delegation for the international committee responsible for developing ISO 20121 (the world's first international and certifiable sustainability management system standard) and a member of the GRI Working Group responsible for developing an Event Organisers Sector Supplement to the GRI G3.1 Sustainability Reporting Guidelines. More recently he was Co-Convenor of the ISO Working Group responsible for drafting competence requirements for auditing and certification of event sustainability management. Since February 2013, Phil has been helping a number of organisations develop and deliver their sustainability policies and strategies whilst looking for his next challenge. He is currently a key member of Kingfisher plc's Net Positive team.

Phil is an outdoor enthusiast and as an experienced hill walker and kayaker tries to get out into the mountains or onto the sea with his (very patient) wife as much as possible.

Acknowledgments

I WOULD LIKE TO THANK everyone who has contributed to this DōShort in so many different ways. As with everything I've written previously, all has been done in what little spare time I have had – in particular the patience of my perhaps far too accepting wife, Jacqui, over the last few months is very much appreciated.

I have encountered many individuals working in the sustainability field who only think about management systems in the context of standards. For some time now I have thought that it would be great to write something on how a management systems approach can help with delivering a sustainability strategy – but from a non-standards view point. Whilst I am absolutely a supporter of standards, I believe they (and the language they use) often get in the way and confuse things. As 2013 has been a big year of change for me, I thought it was as good a time as any to put pen to paper! With this in mind I would firstly like to thank Manda Kiely (BSI), Rhiannon Lewis (Kingston University), Becky Toal (Crowberry Consulting), Julie Duffus (Rio 2016), Claire Buckley (Julie's Bicycle), and Chris Sheldon (Sustainable Events Group) who all commented on the concept for this Short and provided some really helpful encouragement and guidance on how to approach pulling it together.

I would also like to thank the following reviewers and contributors (in no particular order) for providing their much valued thoughts and contributions without which this Short's value would be greatly reduced: Manda Kiely and John Devaney (BSI), Andrew Kinsey (Mace Group),

Catherine Harland, Christina Allen and Becky Coffin (Kingfisher plc), Meegan Jones (GreenShoots Pacific), Beckie Herbert (bdh:sustain), Hayley Baines-Buffery (BioRegional Development Group), Amanda Curtis (Coca-Cola), Andrew Buchanan (Carillion), Eimear Keller (Edelman), Alan Williams and Peter Harris (UPS), Claire Buckley (Julie's Bicycle), Becky Toal (Crowberry Consulting) and Adrian Henriques. I have tried to take on board as many of their comments and contributions as possible. And of course a big thanks to Kingfisher plc and UPS generally for providing supplemental case study material.

I hope I have acknowledged everyone who needed thanking by name but if I've forgotten anyone it's not intentional. Finally, thanks for reading! I hope you find this Short beneficial. Whilst I believe there is no right or wrong answer to how sustainability management should be approached I hope it helps you adopt more sustainable ways of working.

Contents

CHAPTER 1

Introduction

Setting the scene

SO YOU HAVE DEVELOPED an ambitious sustainability vision and strategy and you now need to make this a reality, or perhaps you have lots of interesting initiatives happening on the ground and are struggling to make the link between the two?

Sustainability programmes should not sit apart from the core of how the business is run. They need to be as integrated into the organisation as much as possible. Whilst people are of course key to making things happen, 'hearts and minds' alone are unlikely to deliver your sustainability goals.

Adopting a management systems approach by tapping into and supplementing existing management and governance arrangements will help you to strengthen the link between your sustainability strategy and action. It will support you in implementing more sustainable ways of working and, assuming that there is a positive enabling culture in the organisation, reinforce engagement efforts by making sustainability more relevant to the very individuals you are reaching out to.

The problem is that in many instances as soon as you mention 'management systems' to people their eyes do tend to glaze over. This might be driven through a perception that they are all to do with standards or a view that they are just too overly bureaucratic and technical and only applicable to larger businesses. Neither view is necessarily the case, although granted the language that standards use can get in the way and confuse things for those who aren't too familiar with it.

A number of management system or framework standards relevant to sustainability have emerged in recent years. The ones of particular note are:

- BS 8900-1:2013 and BS 8900-2:2013: Managing sustainable development of organizations[1] (recently revised and now includes a framework for assessment[2]);
- BS ISO 20121:2012: Event sustainability management systems – Requirements with guidance for use[3] (world's first international and certifiable sustainability management system standard – and the approach could be applied to any organisation);
- BS ISO 26000:2010: Guidance on social responsibility[4] (which is quite a heavy read and whilst it is technically not a sustainability standard, it is of some use);
- SIGMA Guidelines[5] (over ten years old but still an incredibly useful resource); and
- Global Reporting Initiative (GRI) G4 Sustainability Reporting Guidelines[6] (a useful resource even you don't intend to actually produce a sustainability report).

You can of course also embed sustainability considerations into more traditional management system standards, such as quality management (e.g. ISO 9001[7]) and environmental management (e.g. ISO 14001[8], although still focusing on the environment the forthcoming revised version of the standard should be much improved and strengthened[9]).

Although you might wish to meet and be independently certified or assessed to one of these standards (where that possibility exists) these should really be secondary considerations. Whilst they do have their place, it is possible to adopt a management systems approach without ever having to follow a single standard.

An earlier DōShort, *Making the Most of Standards – The Sustainability Professional's Guide*[10] provides an insight into the world of sustainability standards. This DōShort provides an introduction to management systems thinking and concepts to help you more effectively deliver on your sustainability ambitions, from a non-standards viewpoint.

Attempts have been made to simplify terminology used in this Short as much as possible. The terms *vision*, *strategy*, *plan*, *policy* and *process* are used throughout. Many organisations will have their own definitions for each of these terms, but for the purposes of this Short they are defined as follows:

Vision	A short, succinct and inspiring forward-looking statement of what an organisation intends to become or achieve at some point in the future. It sets out the future aspirations without saying the why or the how.
Strategy	A high-level document which sets out where you are, what you want to do and where you want to end up. A strategy does not specifically set out how you will achieve this, and instead focuses more on the why – and generally assumes you will be successful. Strategies can exist at different levels of a business – it could be corporate-wide, be specific to a department or team, be operationally focused or specific to a theme (e.g. climate change).

Plan	A plan focuses on the how! For example, it sets out the steps by which you intend to deliver all or aspects of a strategy. It should generally include any interdependencies or assumptions, roles and responsibilities, resource needs, issues and risks, and a clear programme of actions.
Policy	A policy is a clear, concise statement that is endorsed by top management and lays down the rules for something to ensure consistency and compliance with a requirement driven by a strategy and/or plan.
Process	A specified way of carrying out an activity or task that may or may not be documented. Processes may be supported by detailed written procedures or instructions or by other implementation tools. They should generally relate to policies and set out how a policy or aspects of a policy should be implemented.

So what is a management system?

Adopting a management systems approach will help you in being more formalised and systematic in how and when you do things.

A management system provides the means by which your organisation can formalise, document and improve its management practices. It facilitates the delivery of continuous improvement in overall business performance, providing the means for various things (or interventions) to happen. It is not necessarily something you see – it is part of the very fabric of the organisation and what makes it tick.

All businesses will have some form of a management system even if they do not think of it in these terms. They will have policies and processes in place (even if they are not formalised or written down), which amongst other things, will seek to set down rules around how goods and services are procured, how people are hired, how data are collected and managed, or how things are communicated. The management system is essentially the 'sum of all these parts'. How rigorous a particular business is 'directed or controlled' will vary greatly among organisations.

In effect, a good management system should go hand in hand with good organisational governance – they are not mutually exclusive concepts. Many organisations fall down here. They may well have management processes which consider sustainability matters but often have no or limited governance arrangements in place. An important question to answer therefore is how you should best integrate sustainability into key management processes and governance structures of your organisation to ensure effective management oversight and organisational performance. Effective management and governance should mean that you are more likely to achieve your sustainability goals.

The benefits of integrating sustainability into your organisation through a management systems approach include:

- ✓ Establishing a business-wide approach to managing sustainability performance through improved top management ownership and better decision-making;
- ✓ Establishing clear roles and responsibilities for sustainability matters;
- ✓ Enhancing stakeholder engagement, support and partnerships working;

- ✓ Preventing duplicated efforts and overlooking key sustainability issues;
- ✓ Developing the support of sustainability strategies and plans that are consistent with the needs of the business (i.e. are not competing or contradictory);
- ✓ Better planning and allocation of resources;
- ✓ More effective communication of sustainability requirements and achievements;
- ✓ Facilitating coordinated solutions to sustainability issues identified in different areas of the business; and
- ✓ More effective and efficient internal and external assurance and strategic review.

Core principles and structure of this DōShort

You may have heard the phrase Plan Do Check Act (PDCA). Most management system standards are modelled on this concept – known as the Deming Cycle – that originates from the 1950s.[11] This is predicated on modifying a process through continuous feedback that results in an improved and more efficient process over time. The PDCA cycle can be summarised as:

- **Plan**: identifying your vision or goals and developing a strategy;
- **Do**: implementing the plan to deliver your strategy and goals;
- **Check**: monitoring your outcomes and reviewing progress and achievements or problems and areas for improvement; and

- **Act**: acting on the learning derived from the entire process to adjust your goals, change approaches or revise your entire strategy.

The PDCA cycle is not particularly intuitive and some people do struggle with the concept. This is partly because it implies that your approach to developing a management system will always be sequential. In real life, particularly where you have an established business, this will rarely be the case. In reality, you will be doing things out of sequence, often concurrently with other things and in most cases will be continually reviewing and changing things.

The other essential ingredients of any management systems approach is that top management (highest level of management in the organisation) must retain overall ownership and accountability and that key stakeholders are continually engaged and able to feedback their views and thoughts.

In a sustainability context, the key success factors for adopting a management systems approach means that your organisation has:

- ✓ Defined a long-term commitment to sustainability, with a clear vision and goals, and associated programme which has the support of its top management and its key stakeholders;
- ✓ Determined the steps by which progress towards goals will be achieved;
- ✓ Established systems, controls and assurance mechanisms to implement those steps; and
- ✓ Demonstrated progress and improved its overall sustainability performance.

This DōShort aims to help you achieve these key success factors by taking you through each of the following five chapters. Although again this structure implies that the process is sequential, this is not necessarily the case at all. You can dip in and out as is relevant to your circumstances and many things can be done in parallel or out of sequence and the process is iterative. The process should also work for any business, however small or large.

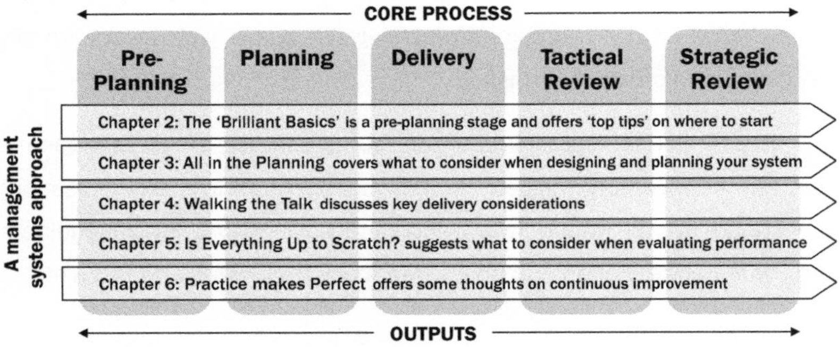

The overall intention of adopting this approach is to help you communicate and build support with peers and senior management, put in place a process to continually improve your sustainability performance, and (should you wish to!) put you in a better position to implement a particular standard.

CHAPTER 2

The 'Brilliant Basics'

Orientation: Where you are in the process

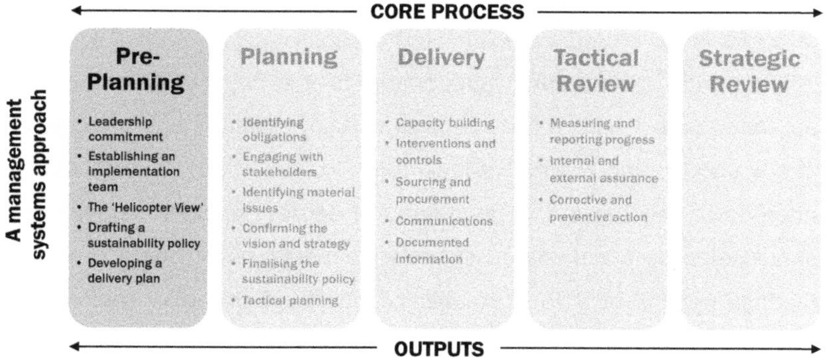

OFTEN OVERLOOKED, there are a number of steps which if implemented well can provide your management system with solid foundations for delivering your sustainability vision and strategy. These steps are known as the 'Brilliant Basics'.

Leadership commitment

It may sound obvious but a solid and genuine commitment from the top is a crucial step towards integrating sustainability into the organisation. This can make or break its potential to become core business.

You should make sure that you have secured the necessary commitment from your top management. You should not assume that this is the case before plunging straight into the planning and delivery phase. Just because you have some sustainability initiatives already in place or possibly even developed a sustainability vision and strategy, does not mean that your organisation's leadership has entirely bought in. Investing time here will save time later on.

When seeking commitment from the top you need to consider how your business is structured. For example, how does a group holding company interact with its operating companies? Is it a command and control approach or is it relatively decentralised? Any commitment needs to be strong enough and at a high enough level to resolve any issues that may arise down the line in the planning and delivery phases. Ideally there should also be a nominated sponsor or champion at board or senior management level – in a smaller organisation this may well be the Managing Director.

This DōShort makes the assumption that your top management is already sold (to an extent anyway) on the business case for sustainability and has some idea of what it wants to achieve that is articulated in the form of a vision and/or a strategy. If this is not the case then an earlier DōShort, *Strategic Sustainability – Why it Matters to Your Business and How to Make It Happen*,[12] outlines why businesses should take action on sustainability. Having said this, at this stage it may only be necessary to prepare an outline business case, vision and strategy. As you progress your understanding you will be able to develop more detailed ones.

Establishing an implementation team

It is not all about top management – involving individuals at all levels of the organisation helps to identify opportunities to drive the management system forward. Leadership can present itself at all levels of your organisation to help build a business-wide approach to sustainability. For example, there could be a key member of staff who may not be all that senior but has been in the organisation for years, is well respected and someone that others listen to – their buy-in is therefore crucial. Spending time understanding and talking to key players in different areas of the business, including who the 'movers and shakers' are and how they work, will pay dividends down the line. 'Bolt-on' initiatives tend to come and go and only those that truly align to core business values and objectives and the culture of the organisation have the ability to last.

For everyone to be bought into sustainability, and for it to become an inherent part of his or her job, is the 'Holy Grail'. Even the best performing companies are unlikely to have reached this level of maturity. The reality is that you will need to establish a 'crack' or core team to drive the process forward and help keep your goals firmly in sight. You could create a separate sustainability department, establish it as a team within a larger department, or simply have an enthusiastic individual supported by representatives from other parts of the business. There is no 'one size fits all' approach to this and will completely depend on how your organisation is set up and organised. Equally this need not necessarily be a large team. A recent survey carried out by ENDS found that almost three-quarters of companies responding had fewer than five full-time equivalent staff in their sustainability teams.[13] Whichever model is chosen for your core team, make sure it has the necessary mandate or 'licence to operate' from top management to avoid it being seen as a side project. You will need good and regular access to your board or senior management sponsor.

At this early stage, begin to outline the roles and responsibilities of those involved in implementing elements of the system, particularly those in top management and the core team. It is also a good idea to consider the resources required to take things forward. For example, what tasks can be done in-house versus those that may require a degree of external resource?

The 'Helicopter View'

Before plunging straight into the detailed design and planning stage it is advisable to take a step back and look at the business from a holistic view and determine its current sustainability performance – essentially this is a high level 'stock-take'.

Try to involve as many people as possible at this stage. Don't fall into the trap of starting with a solution and looking for ways to make it fit. Your mission should be to identify ways to tap into existing company culture, utilise existing processes and structures and amend policies to make sustainability an everyday part of doing business. Undertaking a thorough review of your existing management practices and sustainability performance will help you move towards this.

Think about how your business works and how it interacts with your stakeholders and value chain including areas that are within and outside your direct control or influence. In many respects, as a long-term goal sustainability is about companies accepting their share of responsibility for issues outside their direct control and influence and working with others on common goals. Review your existing or emerging sustainability vision and strategy to identify what commitments you have made or are looking to make. If you are aware of any legal or other requirements of relevance to sustainability make sure these are captured. You may even be aware of your stakeholder views in respect to sustainability matters – capture these as well.

Try and identify programmes or initiatives that are already in place – include all informal or 'ad-hoc' things that are done and those that were introduced but have not hung around. Identify those that are fully aligned with your business strategy and those that are perhaps less so. Many organisations are surprised at how much is already in place although it may not always be seen as contributing to the 'sustainability agenda' (business improvement or efficiency initiatives, for instance). This may also provide you with a great opportunity to educate those internal stakeholders who may not yet fully understand what sustainability is or be completely bought in to what you are attempting to do. It is often helpful to simplify sustainability messages and talk in a language people can relate to and understand.

Identifying the activities that you can and can't control and influence may well require collaboration with other parties. These may not always be very apparent so consider leveraging knowledge and expertise from key staff through one-to-one engagement and workshops. This exercise will help you in setting the boundaries (or scope) of your eventual management system and identifying the major business practice 'interventions' that need to be made.

The key questions to ask during this stage include:

- What are the key business processes and management practices that exist and who owns them?
- What are your organisational values and guiding principles (see below)?
- What are your existing decision-making processes?
- What are the success or failure factors for past initiatives that have been introduced?
- What governance structures and associated processes are in place such as how risks, issues and opportunities are identified and managed?
- How does your performance compare with what your peers are doing? (It is also useful to look at what is going on outside of your sector.)

Organisational values and guiding principles

Most businesses will have a clear purpose, which is understood and shared by their employees, customers and other stakeholders. This purpose should ideally be expressed in the organisation's vision and values and sit at the very heart of the organisation.

A key consideration for your vision and strategy is to adopt a set of guiding principles. These may be informed by your organisation's values if you have them or you could identify your organisation's values from any guiding principles you adopt.

In any event, sustainable development guiding principles help to apply your sustainability strategy in practice by providing reference points for the way in which your organisation should operate and how your employees should be expected to behave.[14]

Commonly held guiding principles of relevance to sustainable development include: inclusivity, integrity, accountability, stewardship, and transparency – there may well be others that you identify though. The following table provides some useful questions to help you reflect on the extent to which your organisation is aligned with these guiding principles:

Guiding principles	Example questions
Inclusivity	• How do you identify those who could affect or be affected by your decisions and actions? • How do stakeholders contribute their views, and is this on a continuing basis? • How do you help stakeholders understand the reasons for the organisation's decisions and implications of its actions? • How can you be sure no groups or individuals are disadvantaged or are 'kept in the dark'? • How is diversity encouraged and developed?

Integrity	• In what ways do you deal with others with integrity? • How do you ensure bribery, abuse, oppression and corruption are avoided? • How do you demonstrate that your decisions and actions are unbiased? • How do you take into account ethical considerations in your decision-making process?
Accountability	• In what ways do you hold yourself account for your actions? • How and to what extent do you account to your stakeholders? • How do you demonstrate that your decisions and actions comply with relevant rights, legal obligations and regulations?
Stewardship	• How do your actions affect quality of life? • Will decisions lead to irreversible environmental or societal change or loss? If so, have alternatives been evaluated? To what extent do you adopt the precautionary principle in decision-making? • In any activity, will the use of resources and its consequent impact be considered and monitored? • How are sustainable development management skills developed, shared, applied and recognised?

Transparency	• How do you make certain that relevant and reliable information is available in an accessible, low-cost and comparable way? • How are reasonable views or requests for further information considered and responded to? • How are significant interests, influences or beneficiaries recorded, communicated and managed? • How can new technologies be used effectively to increase transparency? • How are decision-makers identified and the reasons for decisions recorded and communicated and to whom?

SOURCE: Modified from BS 8900-1:2013.

You should develop a simple way of capturing the outputs of this initial 'Helicopter View' exercise and the key opportunities and gaps that have been identified.

Undertaking a thorough 'stock-take' will provide a solid foundation for your management system and should save you time later on. This stock-take is also something that is advisable to do on a periodic basis and will help you in your strategic review (more on that later).

Drafting a sustainability policy

At this point it is suggested that a sustainability policy is drafted to help provide focus for developing your management system. It does not necessarily have to be seen by anyone outside your business – although it might be sensible to share it with some of your key stakeholders.

During the previous step you should have identified what policies already exist (e.g. environment, health and safety, diversity, etc.) and what commitments you have made or are looking to make. The Sustainability Policy is an overarching policy but does not necessarily replace other existing policies. You should ensure that there are no potential conflicts and consider whether current commitments in other policies still hold true.

During the previous exercise you should have begun to think about, or reaffirm, what the sustainability commitments mean to your organisation. This is because they will be a focus for your management system going forward and will need to be upheld through clear actions. When you eventually come to finalise your policy it will need to be endorsed by your top management (see next chapter).

Developing a delivery plan

The final 'Brilliant Basic' involves preparing a concise overarching delivery plan. This will help bring together a potentially large project in one place and help maintain and track any objectives that were agreed with top management. It will help you communicate how long things will take and how far along you are on the process of implementation.

Drawing on the previous steps, develop a list of everything that needs to be done – this sounds obvious but can often be overlooked. Identify the actions required to implement a full management system, including timescales, milestones, targets or aspirations, and key roles and responsibilities. This plan should be able to be used in a practical way and should be 'live' and evolve over time.

A summary of key 'Brilliant Basics' questions

- Is there a commitment to embed sustainability into your organisation at the highest level? Is everyone fully bought in?
- Has a board level or senior management champion been identified and appointed?
- Does an outline business case for sustainability exist?
- What sustainability ambitions does your top management have for the organisation? Do you understand what it means in the context of your organisation? Is there a shared vision for the organisation?
- What governance structures exist within the organisation? How do or could they relate to sustainability matters?
- Who is responsible for leading on implementation? Have they been given the appropriate 'licence to operate'?
- Do you know what requirements (legal or otherwise) you are obligated to comply with in all locations where you operate?
- What significant or 'material' sustainability issues have been identified and how have they been assessed?
- Have key stakeholders been identified? Are their issues and concerns of relevance to sustainability known?
- What policies, strategies, plans and processes exist within the organisation? How do or could these relate to sustainability?

- What are your organisation's culture, vision and values and how would they support any sustainability programme moving forward? Have you adopted a set of sustainable development guiding principles?
- Are there any individuals or teams that could make or break delivery?
- How have other business-wide programmes been rolled out across the organisation in the recent past? Did these work or not – what were the successes and what were the failures, and why?
- Are roles and responsibilities clearly defined so that decisions can be made and actions taken by the appropriate teams or individuals? Do responsibility assignment matrices exist (a RACI or ARCI matrix)?
- Are the decisions and actions of different parts of the organisation consistent and coordinated? How does or could all this impact sustainability efforts?
- Has a concise overarching delivery plan been prepared which identifies timescales, milestones, key roles and responsibilities and resource needs?

CHAPTER 3

All in the Planning

Orientation: Where you are in the process

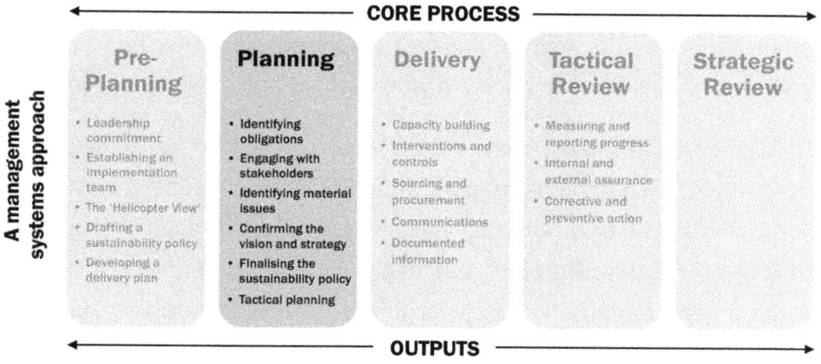

THE PREVIOUS SECTION can be seen as a precursor to this more detailed design and planning stage where the direction of your management system starts to take shape as you decide what needs to be done to improve your sustainability performance.

Identifying obligations

Compliance with the law is step one on the path towards improving your sustainability performance. It is quite common for organisations to commit to becoming more sustainable without ever really having a full appreciation of their local, national and international legal responsibilities. Many of the sustainability issues you will be looking to manage will after all have some form of legal baseline against which you should be looking to exceed in the majority of instances. Further, there is a moral duty on organisations and individuals to comply with the law. How could an organisation claim to be committed to sustainability if they are not in compliance with the law? A confirmed breach of legislation could also completely undermine everything you are setting out to achieve.

Your organisation may also have adopted and committed to complying with other requirements, such as internal corporate standards and policies, contractual requirements, and industry or other best practice codes.

It is important to establish what you are obligated to comply with currently and what might be around the corner in all jurisdictions where you operate. You or others may have already gone through this process to a certain extent. However, this might only be for certain issues (e.g. environment, health and safety, or employment law) and this also may only exist in several areas of your organisation and will not have been pulled together in one place which is what you should be striving for.

Legislative topics to consider include:

- Access to information
- Air quality
- Animal welfare and wildlife protection
- Bribery, corruption and whistleblowing
- Climate change and energy
- Hygiene
- Human rights
- Local environment quality (including noise)
- Marine environments
- Natural and built environment
- Packaging

- Consumer rights
- Contaminated land
- Corporate governance
- Diversity and inclusion
- Employment law
- Hazardous substances
- Health and safety
- Pollution control
- Product safety
- Radioactive substances
- Town and country planning
- Transport
- Waste
- Water

Given the all-embracing nature of the sustainability agenda it will be difficult to find one resource that provides answers to all your legislative questions (a potential gap in the market here perhaps?). Consequently, you will need to draw upon a number of resources to help you do this which range from little to substantial cost. Sources include government websites, industry associations and trade groups, commercial databases and publications (albeit mainly environmental or workplace focused), and professional advisors and consultancy services. Membership of a trade or professional body may also provide you with legal updates and educational opportunities of relevance to sustainable development.

Once you have pulled together all your obligations into one place, ideally a concise register of sorts, it is advisable to determine your level of conformity against each obligation and what improvements may be required. At this stage it is also advisable to consider who will be responsible for managing and updating this register going forward and how key requirements are communicated internally.

CASE STUDY 1 – In practice: Developing a Sustainability Obligations Register

The London Organising Committee of the Olympic Games and Paralympic Games (LOCOG) developed a Sustainability Obligations Register which was reviewed and updated periodically.

The document provided an overview of sustainability related legislation that was directly or indirectly applicable to LOCOG's operations and activities.

A brief summary of legislation and other requirements was included within sections that were organised under subject headings. After each legislative summary, a comment on the potential applicability to LOCOG was provided. An indication of compliance status was also included including whether any further action was required (e.g. need for additional research).

Appendices to this document comprised a matrix of obligations to provide an indication of applicability to LOCOG Departments and Functional Areas. The myriad of planning permissions issued under Town and Country Planning legislation was not included and was held elsewhere within the organisation.

Additional information

- LOCOG Sustainability Obligations Register: **http://learninglegacy.independent.gov.uk/documents/pdfs/sustainability/cp-sustainability-obligations-register.pdf**

Engaging with stakeholders

If compliance with the law is the first step on the path towards improved sustainability, then stakeholder engagement is the path's foundation. The better engaged you are with your stakeholders, the more robust and defensible your sustainability programme is likely to be. Of course, you will already be engaging with a myriad of stakeholders ranging from customers, employees, to suppliers each and every day. But to what extent will you be engaging your stakeholders to seek their views and input on sustainability issues?

Engaging with stakeholders on sustainability matters provides the following benefits by helping you to:

- ✓ Understand what is important to you and them and prioritise issues to manage and what to report;
- ✓ Gain access to additional resource with fresh ideas and expertise which may not exist within your organisation; and
- ✓ Gain buy-in and support which may lead to them to spreading your sustainability messages more widely or supporting you in tough times.

The core steps to helping you achieve these benefits are:

1. Identifying key stakeholders;
2. Effectively engaging with those key stakeholders on an ongoing basis and building mutual trust; and
3. Identifying significant or 'material' sustainability issues with key stakeholders.

All organisations will be involved in stakeholder engagement in one form or another. Customers may be engaged via market research and opinion polls, investors may be engaged through corporate reporting and briefings, employees may be engaged through surveys or worker forums, and there may even be forums for specialist stakeholders on specific topics. The priority should be to identify all engagement activities and bring them all together.

The next step is to undertake a stakeholder mapping exercise to identify who is being engaged and who isn't but needs to be. You will need to understand their views and interests, how they relate to your sustainability programme and other stakeholders, and then determine how relevant they are to you and identify material issues.

Many organisations identify their stakeholders by category as there are many potential different groups, for example, employees, NGOs, customers and investors, but this may not always be realistic as many individuals either may not fit into any category or may overlap into a number of groups. For example, an employee may also be a customer and an investor.

The following provides an indicative list of stakeholder groups:

Business	Government	Societal
• Top management • Employees • Unions • Investors • Customers • Suppliers • Trade associations • Competitors	• Government departments • Local authorities • Emergency and security services • Regulatory agencies and authorities • QUANGOs	• Residents • Local community interest groups • Non-governmental organisations (local and global) • Research institutions • Press and media

It is likely to be impossible to engage with every group of stakeholders, so in identifying your key ones consider the following questions:

- Which stakeholders engage regularly with your organisation?
- Which stakeholder groups are well represented and which ones less so?
- Which stakeholders have information or expertise on an issue that could be helpful to you?
- Which stakeholders have significant influence and who with (e.g. your peers, NGOs, general public, investors, etc.)?
- Which stakeholders have a legal right to be consulted?
- Which stakeholders could derail or challenge the credibility of your programme if they are not engaged?

You may need to undertake several stakeholder mapping exercises for different aspects of your sustainability programme: for example, identifying those key stakeholders who have an interest in your wider business versus those who may only have an interest in a particular issue (e.g. supply chain labour standards). Use of an interest/influence matrix may aid this process (Figure 1).

It is a good idea to develop an overarching stakeholder engagement strategy which summarises the engagement process in your organisation. This should capture those established engagement processes that are an inherent part of your business and those mechanisms you need to introduce to specifically support your sustainability programme. This should be supported by a stakeholder engagement plan which sets out

FIGURE 1. Interest/influence stakeholder matrix.

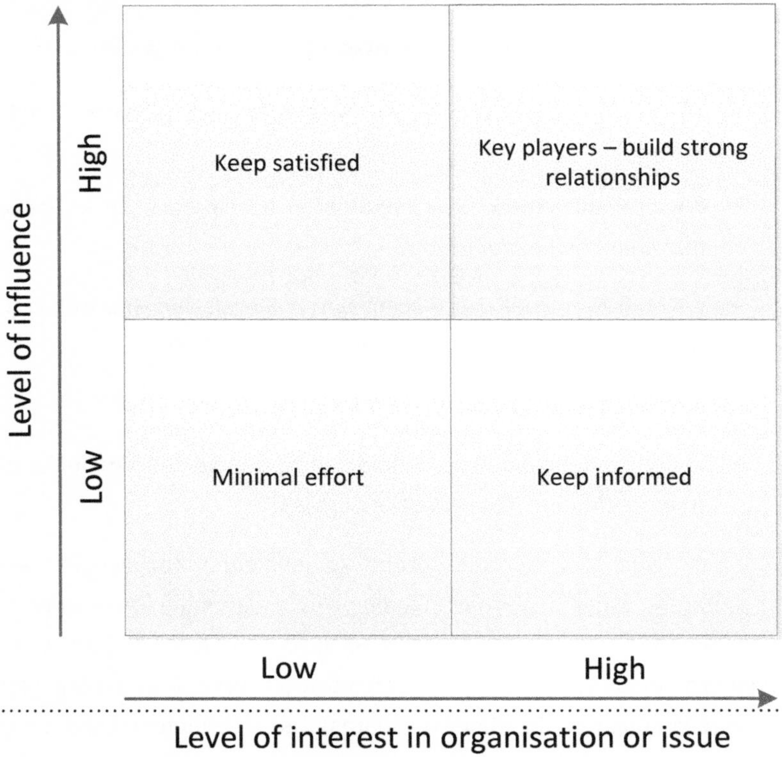

SOURCE: Adapted from Mendelow's Matrix[15]

the how the strategy will be delivered, including key tasks and timelines, engagement leads, channels of communication and engagement outputs and outcomes (more on this later). The strategy and plan will need to be regularly reviewed and revised to ensure ongoing representation of relevant groups and individuals.

Further guidance on stakeholder identification and engagement is available in BS 8900-1:2013 and AA1000 Stakeholder Engagement Standard (AA1000SES).[16]

Identifying material issues

At some point in the process you are likely to end up with a long list of issues identified as part of your own internal reviews or raised by your stakeholders. It may be difficult to separate out the issues that should receive the most attention. Identifying the 'material' issues that are of greatest importance to your organisation and your stakeholders is key to moving forward. Knowledge and understanding of what your significant issues are is a must when developing your sustainability vision and strategy.

Start by developing a comprehensive list of issues identified as part of the 'Helicopter View' stage and undertaking additional internal research. There is no right or wrong approach to identifying and classifying issues. Issues may be classified according to themes and subjects (e.g. climate change, waste, inclusion or human rights) or sub-topics (e.g. climate change adaptation, recycling, employment and skills, or labour standards). Many issues will not be able to be readily classified solely as fitting into an environmental, social or economic category because they are often cross-cutting (food, for example). Issues may also be identified by other means such as risk registers (potential and dynamic risks), incident reporting processes, audits, and of course most importantly the views of your stakeholders!

In addition to looking at what your peers have done a simple Internet search will throw up a huge number of checklists, guidelines and other resources which may help you in this process. Examples include the SIGMA Guidelines Guide to Sustainability Issues,[17] the UN Global Compact's 10 Principles,[18] the GRI Sustainability Reporting Guidelines or the One Planet Living Principles framework.[19] However, whilst all these may help you identify a potential issue they will not help you in determining its significance, neither is it likely that they will identify all the issues that may be relevant to your business. Only you will know your issues as they should relate specifically to your unique situation.

Whatever method is chosen for identifying your issues, it should be as consistent as possible and be clear on how your materiality evaluation took place. Points to consider include:

- What is the scale, severity and duration of the issue?
- Is the issue controlled by legislation?
- Have your stakeholders identified the issue as a concern?
- Do you have control or influence over the issue?
- Are you willing to accept some responsibility for an issue which is outside your direct control or influence and work collaboratively with others on common goals?
- Is it an actual or potential issue?
- Does the issue represent a risk reputational issue or opportunity?
- Is the issue positive (beneficial) or negative (adverse)?
- Does the issue result in a permanent or temporary impact?
- Is the issue of local or global significance?
- How probable is it that the issue will occur?

It is difficult to get the right balance between having a robust approach to identifying your material issues and getting too carried away. Take a step back every now and then to ensure you are not missing the obvious, or focusing on something that is really not that important.

Once you have a list of what you think are your most material issues you need to corroborate this by seeking views from your key stakeholders. This is an ongoing and iterative (and at times painful) process. Whilst you may think an issue is important or not important you should not assume your stakeholders will see things in the same way. You will need to evaluate each issue according to the level of stakeholder concern (taking account of the previous mapping considerations) and impact on your business (for example, the issue may be key to delivering your sustainability programme). Unfortunately, you may find yourself in the position of being pressured into addressing something, which is seen of utmost importance to your stakeholders, but in the grand scheme of things as far as you are concerned there are bigger fish to fry.

Finally, consider reviewing your material issues in the context of whether they are:

- Issues that are relevant to the entire organisation and need to be addressed and communicated at a corporate level (strategic issues); or
- Issues that are relevant or specific to a department or team or are work stream-specific (tactical issues).

In the case of the latter, given the narrower scope of departments, teams or work streams compared to your organisation as a whole material issues should be reviewed and rationalised based on relevance to enable tactical plans, objectives or targets to be developed if necessary.

CASE STUDY 2 – In practice: Determining materiality

A key criticism of the first London 2012 Sustainability Report, published in April 2011, was the lack of an executive summary or weighting of the issues covered by its sustainability programme. The sheer number of issues that were covered left many stakeholders wanting.

Consequently LOCOG conducted a materiality review to improve its understanding of stakeholders' expectations and to ensure these were reflected in its sustainability efforts and reporting. A representative group of London 2012 stakeholders including the wider public were consulted through three main phases of activity:

1. Internal review: collation and review of all relevant internal sustainability data including core sustainability themes, subjects and issues and existing impact and risk assessments;
2. External review: stakeholders representative of its 12 stakeholder groups (over 700 individuals) were engaged around a long list of sustainability issues through either a publicly available online survey, surveys of the public undertaken by Nielsen, or in-depth telephone interviews. From this a shortlist of issues were extracted which stakeholders commonly identified as a priority to them; and
3. Prioritisation: key stakeholders were engaged around a shortlist of sustainability issues through several workshops

and conducted an internal review to review the outcomes and prioritise the set of material issues.

This proved to be an immensely useful exercise and LOCOG could have benefited from doing this much earlier in its lifecycle.

Stakeholders identified six sustainability issues for London 2012 to prioritise in its communications and engagement:

- Carbon: using carbon footprinting as a tool to deliver a low-carbon Games;
- Employment in business: using the Games as a platform for showcasing the economic benefit of sustainability;
- Promoting sustainable living: how sustainability will be made a visible part of the Games;
- Travel and transport: provision of more sustainable travel and transport solutions;
- Waste: delivering a zero waste (to landfill) Games; and
- Olympic Park: regenerating the communities of east London.

Consequently, for the Pre-Games Sustainability Report in April 2012 a summary report was prepared focussing on these priority issues. They were also highlighted through case studies and stakeholder perspectives throughout the main report. In addition, the main report addressed programme delivery and GRI requirements.

Confirming the vision and strategy

As previously stated, this DōShort makes the assumption that you already have a sustainability vision and strategy or at least have a pretty good idea what they should be. Drawing on all the previous steps, at this point in the process it is advisable to review and confirm that they are still appropriate for your organisation, and if not, revise accordingly.

For instance, to what extent does your sustainability vision and strategy relate to your organisation's overall vision, values and business strategy? Ultimately they should not sit apart and should be integrated. Further, to what extent does it address your material or significant sustainability issues, the needs and expectations of your stakeholders, and support your organisation to operate in accordance with widely accepted sustainable development guiding principles (see 'Brilliant Basics' chapter)?

Other key considerations when reviewing your vision and strategy include:

- How receptive the culture of your organisation is to what is being proposed and what changes may be required?
- What other business-wide strategies exist and whether there are any conflicts?
- What goals in the short (up to five years), medium (five to 20 years) and long term (20+ years) are you looking to set (see below)? How do they relate to your material issues?
- Where do you want your organisation (or parts of it) to be by a given date and what timescales should it be working towards?

- What is your scope or boundaries? What issues are you willing or not willing to accept responsibility for? Do your strategy and goals apply to all parts of your organisation or only certain bits of it? How do these align with the views of your stakeholders?
- To what extent will you engage and consult with your key stakeholders on your vision and strategy?

Establishing goals

There is no set way of establishing goals but they could take the form of:

- **Aims** – what you want to achieve;
- **Objectives** – what you will do to specifically meet the aim; and
- **Targets** – outcomes(s) that need to be met in order to achieve a particular objective.

Not all organisations set goals but they can be an incredibly powerful engagement tool for your top management, your employees and your wider stakeholders. They can be a great way to focus attention and create a shared ambition for everyone to buy into and work towards. Goals should ideally be stretching yet also achievable and measurable (see next chapter).

You will also need to consider whether your targets will be absolute or relative, as follows:

- **Absolute targets** – are hard and fast and are a direct measure of performance regardless of any variables (changes in the business) although there may be an established baseline or reference scenario against which progress will be measured (e.g. X% reduction in absolute carbon footprint (tonnes CO_2e) from a 2012/13 baseline); and
- **Relative targets** – are normalised according to variables, i.e. they take account of year-on-year changes taking place in the business (e.g. reduce CO_2 emissions by X% per product produced between April 2012 and March 2016)

As to which approach to take, it is not necessarily straightforward and will require careful consideration and discussion. On the one hand an absolute target may constrain an organisation particularly if it is in a period of growth, and on the other, relative targets may open you up to stakeholder criticism if they are considered to be a 'cop-out'.

Goals can be set over a variety of timescales – for instance, you might have a long-term target and wish to set short- to medium-term milestones or other performance indicators to gauge how you're progressing. Again look at how other organisations have approached this – your peers and those outside your industry – and seek the views of your stakeholders as they will also no doubt have a view too.

Ideally you should be in a position to finalise or reaffirm your sustainability vision and strategy and seek the appropriate endorsements from top management.

Finalising the sustainability policy

You will ideally have prepared a draft sustainability policy earlier in the process (see 'Brilliant Basics' chapter). You should also now be in a position to finalise it and seek top management endorsement and then communicate it to your employees, supply chain and wider key stakeholders.

This written 'statement of intent' should outline your organisation's sustainability vision and is what should drive the whole of the management system. When finalised it should become a publicly available declaration of your intentions and commitment to improving your sustainability performance. In many ways it is a 'contract' made between your organisation and its stakeholders.

A typical sustainability policy should include the broad sustainability commitments and intentions of your organisation and be between one and two sides of A4. It should make reference to your strategy, your sustainability priorities and long-term goals, and what you intend to do to fulfil your commitments.

You should ensure that the policy truly reflects what you intend to do. It should be signed off by top management and dated.

Avoid the use of jargon or statements that you cannot substantiate (e.g. avoid using the term 'environmentally friendly').

Try and keep the policy general enough to avoid the need for frequent alterations and reissues although it will of course need to be reviewed on a periodic basis.

Tactical planning

Once finalised and endorsed by top management your sustainability vision and strategy should provide your organisation with a roadmap of what it wants to achieve by when. However, no matter how robust your high-level strategy is it will not be enough to provide your organisation with everything that is required to secure its delivery.

You will need to firm up what needs to be done and identify what else is required with regards supporting strategies, plans, policies and processes, and so on. These may be business-wide (e.g. a Carbon Strategy), specific to an issue (e.g. a Packaging Policy), department or team specific (e.g. a Logistics Sustainability Plan), simply embedding a requirement in a business process or any combination thereof. This enables different parts of your organisation to contribute via different actions to the same overall goal or goals. The eventual approach will of course very much depend on the nature and scale of the business.

You may also need to embed sustainability considerations into other organisational processes that are in place (e.g. procurement, information systems, training and development, recruitment, and so on) (see next chapter).

Whatever approach or approaches are chosen it is important to ensure that everything is clear to all individuals who need to be involved in delivery. The 'Helicopter View' exercise should have provided you with a good insight into how your organisation is managed and what governance arrangements exist (or don't, as the case may be). Key questions to consider at this stage include:

- What is your approach to supply chain management including tender evaluation and contract management?
- What existing business processes do you need to 'tap into' or what further mechanisms need to be introduced?
- Which departments and teams are high sustainability priorities versus those of lesser priority including which ones are more engaged than others (teams and senior managers)?
- What are your organisational objectives, targets and performance indicators and who is responsible for monitoring and recording progress against them?

It might be useful to consider looking at your organisation from different viewpoints to identify whether an 'intervention' is required to facilitate something to happen – or at least enable certain questions to get asked. For example, does a department and teams need its own delivery strategy, plan, objectives and targets or does it simply get picked up as part of a business-wide process (e.g. procurement) should the need arise.

This review may result in a degree of repetition but that's fine and you can simply skip over and move onto the next. These different viewpoints may include:

- Departments and teams;
- Procurement categories;
- Business processes;
- Current objectives and targets;

- Current risks and opportunities; and/or
- Client group or key stakeholder group expectations.

Systematically looking at each of the above in turn in the context of your sustainability programme and goals will help identify key themes and trends; synergies to avoid any duplication of effort; 'movers and shakers' who can make or break your plans; risks and opportunities; who needs to do what; skills and competency requirements; and gaps that need plugging. It will also help you to underpin your strategy and identify and prioritise your short-term actions – you cannot possibly address everything! Not initially anyway...

By this time it will also be necessary to review and revise your overarching delivery plan (see 'Brilliant Basics' chapter) if you have not done so already with updated actions (identified from the above), milestones, roles and responsibilities and resource needs.

CHAPTER 4

Walking the Talk

Orientation: Where you are in the process

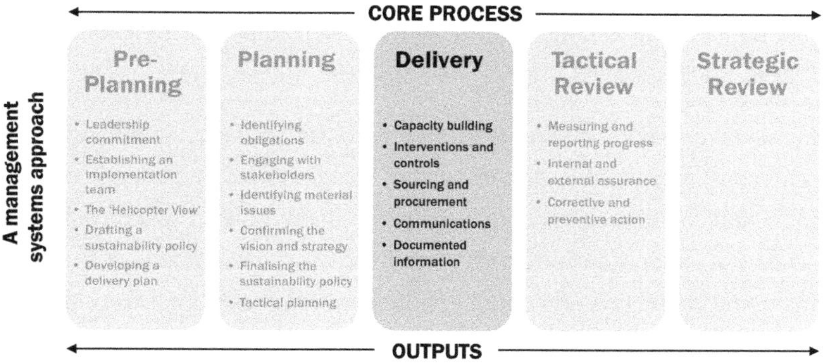

THIS IS WHERE A MANAGEMENT SYSTEMS APPROACH starts to come into its own as your planned actions begin to exert a level of control and influence over the activities of your organisation to improve its sustainability performance. This is easier said than done and whilst you're striving for a more coordinated and consistent approach throughout the organisation this will be very difficult to achieve and will take time.

Capacity building

It probably goes without saying that the success of your sustainability strategy and supporting management system will be heavily dependent on:

- How competent, engaged and motivated your staff are; and
- How well you're able to leverage additional resources

Whilst roles and responsibilities for specific tasks should ideally have been agreed (or in advanced discussion at the very least) by this stage individuals may not necessarily have all the knowledge and skills. It is a good idea to review their training needs to ensure that they are able to carry out their tasks. Training needs may also be identified for senior management as well. Whilst this may seem obvious it is often something that is overlooked.

Ideally you should be seeking to incorporate your sustainability vision into your recruitment and induction programmes including relevant individual job descriptions. Sustainability issues should also be included as part of your organisation's core training and development programme including inductions and appraisals, however formal or informal. Perhaps also consider introducing some 'carrots' by including sustainability as part of your organisation's reward and recognition arrangements. People will generally respond better when they know how sustainability fits in with their other priorities. It is notable that several leading organisations, including Kingfisher plc,[20] Marks and Spencer[21] and IKEA,[22] are introducing these types of incentives as part of their strategies.

It could be argued that the amount of resource an organisation commits to provide is indicative of how seriously it takes the sustainability agenda. Whilst there is possibly some truth in this, if things go well there may only be need for an initial upfront investment. This does not necessarily mean that there will be significant ongoing costs though. Improving operational efficiencies will hopefully give rise to cost savings (such as energy conservation measures), safeguard the business against rising costs (such as strategic sourcing opportunities), or other revenue opportunities (such as sharing recycling revenues with your waste contractor). As your organisation matures new market opportunities will hopefully present themselves.

You will need to tap into a range of resources to help you achieve your sustainability goals. These additional resources may include:

- Additional staff or staff with specific expertise;
- Training and development of key individuals or teams;
- Infrastructure;
- Specialist professional or consultancy services;
- Specialist technology;
- Budget for additional R&D; and
- Contingency budgets for 'what if' scenarios.

These additional resources need not always come at a direct cost to your business. There are a number of avenues that could be explored in this respect, for example:

- Leveraging government resources for advice, training and awareness (e.g. in the UK this could be the Technology Strategy Board, the Waste & Resources Action Programme [WRAP], or in England the Manufacturing Advisory Service);
- Participating in collaborative programmes with other organisations or suppliers to share knowledge and technology;

- Participating in industry or trade forums to identify and address common issues, share experiences, engage external resources, and so on;
- Exploring whether you are eligible to apply for any grant funding;
- Establishing links with professional bodies or networking associations (e.g. the Global Association of Corporate Sustainability Officers), universities or other academic institutions;
- Identifying and reviewing existing industry specific sustainability education initiatives such as lessons learned case studies, webinars, workshops, and so on; and
- Identifying what support your stakeholders may be able to provide at no or limited cost (e.g. provision of specialist secondees), particularly if there is a mutual legacy benefit.

The organisation's knowledge and understanding will continue to evolve as your strategy and management system evolves. There will be considerable lessons learned (i.e. what went well, or what didn't go well) and it is important that attempts are made to capture this learning to enable opportunities for innovation and performance improvements to be identified. This can be a challenge for any business - no matter how small or large they are. You might think a small organisation will find this relatively easy - this is not necessarily the case. Knowledge can unfortunately be quite territorial and coveted and one of the bigger challenges will be to access what is likely to be incredibly useful information. This may take a considerable amount of time. Again this reinforces the need to have a good understanding of the prevailing organisational culture and the 'movers and shakers' that could make or break your efforts. Granted though, the bigger the organisation the harder this will be to do so investigate tapping into knowledge management arrangements where they exist.

CASE STUDY 3 – In practice: Developing leaders and connecting people

Kingfisher plc is Europe's leading home improvement retail group and the third largest in the world with over 1,000 stores in nine countries in Europe and Asia.

Kingfisher's purpose is to create 'Better Homes, Better Lives'. This means making it easier for customers to have better and more sustainable homes. Their programme of eight strategic initiatives to achieve this purpose is called 'Creating the Leader'.

In October 2012, Kingfisher launched Net Positive, which is their ambition to contribute positively to some of the big challenges facing the world, while creating a more valuable and sustainable business for their stakeholders. Net Positive is one of the eight specific steps that make up 'Creating the Leader'.

Kingfisher sees Net Positive as a huge opportunity to develop the way they work and a chance to inspire and involve people around the business. Each of their 80,000 employees across the organisation has the potential to become a Net Positive pioneer.

Training programmes are being launched to help improve the knowledge base within their companies and empower employees to create change. They are focusing first on their most senior employees, who need to show leadership on Net Positive and will play an essential role in engaging their teams. For example, a new module on Net Positive is being developed for their 'One Academy', the development programme for their leadership team. They are also integrating Net Positive into the performance management systems and bonus criteria for key employees.

Under the ethos of working as 'One Team' intelligent networks have been established for employees to interact, share ideas and move easily around the Group, so that knowledge and talent can be placed where it makes the biggest difference. The Kingfisher Net Positive Network is one of these networks. It is made up of the Group Net Positive team and cross-functional representatives from each Operating Company. It meets twice a year in person and through quarterly webinars. It is a forum for reviewing progress and sharing ideas, learnings and best practices.

Additional information

- Net Positive Launch Report: **http://www.kingfisher.co.uk/netpositive/files/downloads/kingfisher_netpos_brochure.pdf**
- Net Positive Report 2012/13: **http://www.kingfisher.co.uk/netpositive/files/reports/cr_report_2013/2013_Net_Positive_Report.pdf**

Interventions and controls

A number of processes will exist within your organisation at different levels ranging from the very basic such as posting an item of mail to the more complex such as planning and launching a new product or service. You will want to exert a level of control and influence over the activities of your organisation. Therefore, it is extremely important to identify what 'interventions' are required to ensure sustainability matters are considered as part of day-to-day business activities. This is of course easier said than done and is often the weakest link for many organisations when attempting to deliver their sustainability strategy. There is often a gulf that exists between the strategy itself and the goals it aspires to achieve or there may be some processes but no clear governance or escalation arrangements in place.

By this stage you should understand how your organisation ticks and how positive and receptive the prevailing culture is – and if you don't then come up with a plan to address any unanswered questions.

Hopefully you will have mapped out your key business processes and controls and how they relate to each other as part of the 'Helicopter View' stage (see 'Brilliant Basics' chapter) and have done more detailed planning to identify what needs to be done including amending any processes and addressing any gaps (see 'All in the planning' chapter). Internal engagement is critical here because you are likely to receive a degree of resistance from people who:

- Developed the process originally and are very proud of what they have done and not minded to alter it; or
- Have always done things in a certain way and are resistant to change.

You will need to take a comprehensive look at your organisation and identify the things you really need to control and manage. It will be necessary to be at your most diplomatic and constructively challenge the norm. For instance, why has something been done in a certain way? Who actually owns the process? Who originally signed the process off – or has something simply become a way of working by default? Does a responsibility assignment matrix exist (a RACI or ARCI matrix) for the process, are individuals with sustainability responsibilities identified, and if not should they be?

With any organisation processes may be simplistically categorised as follows:

1. **Management processes:** the overarching arrangements that set out how an organisation is run and how decisions are made;
2. **Operational processes:** those which are core to what the business is all about such as procurement, research and development, design, manufacturing, service delivery, logistics, customer services, marketing and sales, and so on; and
3. **Support processes:** those which support and underpin the running of the business such as finance, HR, IT, legal, risk assurance, internal audit, communications and public affairs, investor relations, and so on.

Not all processes will necessarily need to include consideration of sustainability matters. You will need to identify, and in some instances prioritise, the processes that are most critical to influence. This will very much depend on your sustainability strategy and the goals you are looking to achieve.

In all instances you should be asking yourself the following in the context of 'business as usual' and what happens in extreme circumstances (e.g. when things might go wrong):

- Is there a sustainability 'angle' to the process and is it important to your strategy and goals?
- Is an existing process appropriate and adequate from a sustainability standpoint – can decisions be made without any consideration of sustainability at all? Is the process consistently applied throughout the organisation or are there inconsistencies (e.g. some teams follow it and some do not)? What happens when things go wrong which may necessitate mitigation and response actions?
- Does an existing process or 'intervention' need to be modified to improve consideration of sustainability matters? What needs to be done to improve consistent application throughout the organisation?
- Is a new process or 'intervention' required?

Controls may also be necessary to support a process. These may include policies, documented procedures or work instructions, management plans (e.g. Environmental Management Plans), contracts or supplier agreements (see next section), use of trained personnel, or formal committees or sub-committees with decision-making powers. Figure 2 provides an illustrative example of where controls or interventions may be inserted into a building or infrastructure design development which follows the RIBA Plan of Work 2013[23] process up to the construction stage.

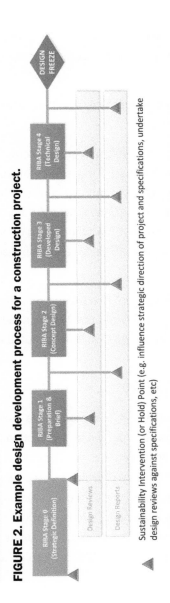

FIGURE 2. Example design development process for a construction project.

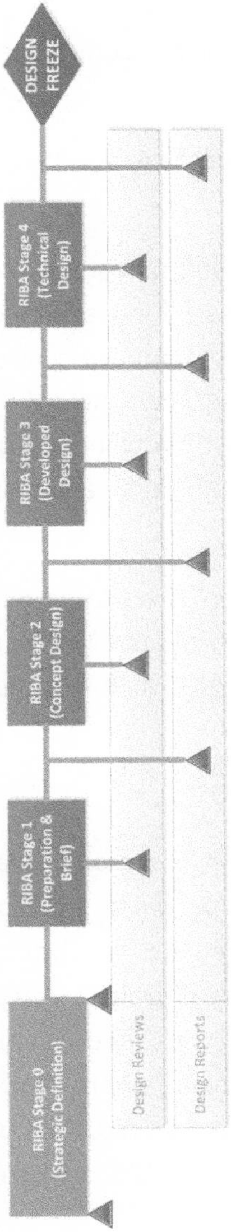

Sustainability Intervention (or Hold) Point (e.g. influence strategic direction of project and specifications, undertake design reviews against specifications, etc)

Reporting and escalation is another area that needs to be considered. For example, what do you do if a process is not being followed, you reach an impasse with an individual or team, or you need to deviate from an agreed policy position? Does a formal route of escalation exist for a business decision to be made and how high should this go?

There is no single or right or wrong approach to introducing critical interventions and establishing controls. It is about determining the best approach for your organisation which is in keeping with the prevailing culture, making sure roles and responsibilities are clear (e.g. whom the buck stops with, who is the doer, who needs to be formally consulted, and whom needs to be kept in and out of the loop), and a clear route of escalation exists where necessary.

Effective engagement with individuals and teams is crucial. They are likely to know how things work far better than you. Often it may be a case of setting out where you want to get to and they will suggest what will work best.

CASE STUDY 4 – In practice: Sustainability interventions

Two key areas of focus for UPS are the mitigation of climate change and urban (air quality, noise and congestion) challenges. In order to address these areas, UPS first looks at the efficiency of operations, then assesses where alternative technologies and mitigation activities can be applied. All investment proposals are sponsored by a functional group with support from the regional Director of Sustainability. These proposals are then run through a capital investment approval process which includes input from management at District, Region and Corporate levels.

As an official partner of the London 2012 Games, UPS took LOCOG's sustainability mission to its core, by getting the necessary investment approval to introduce a range of technologies and measures. This included investing in ten biomethane-diesel vehicles, two electric and three hybrid electric vehicles to its London fleet, as well as introducing an innovative telematics system which helped drivers optimise routes and reduce energy consumption. UPS's fleet for the London 2012 Olympics also included 20 electric vehicles operating out of UPS's Camden and Barking facilities. Post-Games, all of the alternative fuel vehicles have been deployed within their wider UK Network providing a longer-term benefit. This was made possible through the use of the Games as a testing ground for the integration of new, more sustainable fuel technologies into UPS's existing logistics network.

In addition, bicycles and walkers were introduced to help cope with the heightened traffic and a barge carried 38 containers of furniture for the Athlete's Village on the River Thames in London, which had seen little or no commercial barge traffic for decades. Any residual climate change impact was mitigated through the purchase of Gold Standard carbon offsets, in partnership with the CarbonNeutral Company.

For UPS, sponsoring the 2012 Games provided some vital lessons which allowed them to improve day-to-day operations. The telematics technology proved difficult due to unpredictable security delays at venue entrances which meant that it was difficult to control idling time. UPS noted that in a normal operation with more repeatability, the telematics technology would bring great efficiency benefits, as has been shown in UPS's operation in the US. UPS are now pushing ahead with the deployment of this technology to all of UPS's UK-based collection and delivery fleet by the end of 2014.

The mitigation methodology that UPS applied to the Games is available to all customers in the UK through UPS Carbon Neutral. A recent grant from the European Commission is also allowing UPS to upgrade their existing fleet with alternative fuel technology. By the end of 2017, UPS is aiming to reset its goal for miles driven in alternative fuel/advanced technology vehicles to one billion miles globally – more than double their previous goal.

Sourcing and procurement

The way in which your organisation spends its money (headcount, running costs and overheads, and operational expenditure) is a useful way to help you identify and prioritise your sustainability efforts. The balance of this expenditure will clearly vary from organisation to organisation.

As an operational expenditure, sourcing and procurement of goods and services has the potential to have significant impacts. However, if you integrate sustainability considerations into procurement methods and processes it can be used to make positive contributions to your sustainability strategy and associated goals.

For many organisations delivery of their sustainability goals will be heavily dependent on their supply chain and may be the single biggest sustainability intervention that should be made.

This may appear to be a daunting task because your procurement activity may involve hundreds or thousands of individual purchases from a wide range of suppliers. Prioritisation is key and you will need to determine which parts of your sustainability programme are dependent on your supply chain being able to support or deliver.

Come up with a set of key prioritisation criteria (e.g. an own brand good; significant use of labour; level of reputational risk/stakeholder concern; ability to control or influence; ability to contribute to objectives and targets, and so on) and identify those 'priority spend areas' to focus on and determine what is required. For example, is it to challenge a supplier on how they might supply goods and services in a more sustainable way, or are you requiring them to meet a certain standard or requirement (supplying FSC certified timber, for instance). Give careful thought to what you ideally require and what is a 'must have' versus a 'nice to have'. You might also wish to prepare a matrix setting out all your procurement categories and what is expected or proposed for each.

Advance market intelligence and engagement is advisable for a number of reasons. You might simply want to understand the current market and what more sustainable options may exist, or you may want to give the industry a 'heads up' of what you are looking for. This 'forward commitment' approach can lead to significant sustainability wins. For example, the Olympic Delivery Authority engaged with their supply chain to develop more sustainable concrete mixes resulting in a saving of approximately 30,000 tonnes (24%) of embodied carbon and elimination of over 70,000 road vehicle emissions.[24] Another excellent example is where the HM Prison Service used a forward commitment approach to procure a Zero Waste Mattress and Pillow Solution.[25]

You will need to consider how formalised your sourcing and procurement process is or needs to be. For example, how formalised is your tendering process when selecting suppliers or do you follow a relatively 'light of touch' process? Sustainability requirements should ideally be fully incorporated into the core tender specification – if they are seen to sit apart this may encourage the supplier to place a 'premium' on what they propose to supply. Regardless of approach you should still have clear criteria when evaluating prospective bidders on sustainability matters.

If you are already in an existing long-term contractual relationship with a supplier you may feel you are limited in what you can ask of them – do not be afraid to do so though. If they are resistant then determine what existing break clauses or change control provisions are present in the contract or simply identify when the contract is up for renewal and prioritise accordingly.

Sourcing and procurement arrangements will vary with any given organisation including who is responsible and who is consulted or only informed. Sourcing requirements may also sit in different areas of the organisation. For example, product specific requirements may sit with a specialist buying team whereas responsibility for reviewing compliance against working conditions minimum standards at manufacturing locations may reside with a completely separate team. Procurement teams may be responsible for reviewing both technical and commercial requirements, or only commercial aspects. In a smaller organisation procurement responsibilities are likely to rest with individuals who have lots of other responsibilities.

Sustainability clauses should be included in your standard terms and conditions and there should also be provision to introduce additional requirements where necessary (e.g. as a supporting schedule). For example, even if your chosen supplier has provided an excellent tender response this will not be contractually binding unless it is referred to in some way in contract. A supplier proposal is simply a glorified marketing document unless is it is contractualised – this is a surprisingly common pitfall many organisations stumble into.

Consideration should also be given to what provisions are in place or required in the event of a dispute. This could occur where a supplier has simply not met a product requirement (e.g. the timber it is supplying is determined to not have full FSC chain of custody) or where you become aware of an issue at a site producing goods for you (e.g. allegations have been made about breaches in international labour standards such as poor welfare conditions or use of underage workers). Again, it is surprisingly common to find that many contracts are finalised without any thought to dispute resolution. Of course, even if you have such provisions in place you will need to determine how robust they would be if ever relied upon in practice (seek legal opinion if possible!). Further, walking away from a supplier relationship should always be the last resort after all other attempts have been made to resolve the issue.

It will be necessary to produce additional policies and tools to support any supply chain engagement efforts. Historically some organisations have produced generic responsible procurement policies or produced 'codes of conduct' which may be relatively narrow in focus (such as stipulating minimum labour standards). These may also be supplemented by other requirements. There appears to be a move towards integrating product and production site requirements in the form of more prescriptive supplier codes including greater emphasis on the need for supply chain transparency. For example, LOCOG produced a Sustainable Sourcing Code to support its sourcing and procurement activities (see Case Study 5 below) and Sainsbury's is in the process of developing its own Sustainable Sourcing Code to support its 20 x 20 sustainability plan.[26]

Figure 3 brings the above altogether with a suggested approach to embedding sustainability into the procurement process.

A few words of caution though. Having well thought-out supplier selection processes and getting requirements embedded into contract is actually the (relatively) easy part. Getting a supplier to deliver fully in accordance with their obligations is an entirely different matter. Your approach to contract management is an area which needs some careful thought and should be considered when prioritising which spend areas to focus your efforts on.

FIGURE 3. Overview of an approach to sustainable procurement.

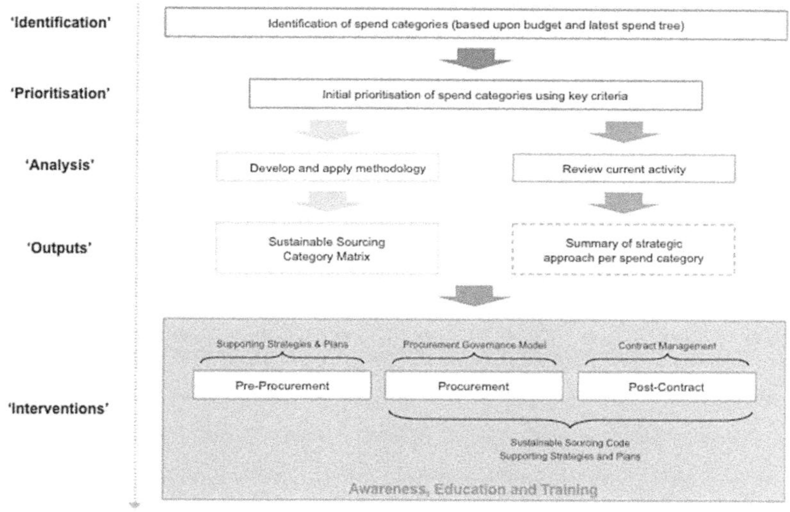

SOURCE: LOCOG.

Your procurement team may not have any contract management skills and other teams in the organisation may not have either.

This may be compounded by the fact that the supplier just simply does not have the capability or capacity to deliver your requirements. If a supplier promises you the earth on sustainability but is not really doing much off its own back this should be a red flag! Whilst it is right that businesses should look to place more stringent sustainability requirements on their suppliers they should also be encouraging them to develop their own strategies and plans as well. When asked if a supplier has their own sustainability strategy or plan they will often say no and simply say that this is because they respond to client requirements. This is of course nonsense – it is possible for a supplier to develop their own sustainability strategy and plan to address their material issues which can also accommodate client specific requirements. In the event of a conflict in policy there can at least be an 'eyes wide open' discussion. Rather this than simply saying yes to a client requirement in full knowledge that there is likely to be a bit of a car crash down the road. Encouraging your suppliers to develop their own strategies and plans will enable them to build their own capability and capacity and be in a better position to respond to your needs in the long run.

Sustainable sourcing and procurement is an emerging discipline both as a process and as a profession and there is a huge wealth of material starting to become available. This DōShort has attempted to provide an introduction to this subject and how it fits into a management systems approach and your armoury of 'interventions'. A Guidance Standard BS 8903 'Principles and framework for procuring sustainably' was published in 2010[27] and more recently the Chartered Institute of Purchasing and Supply have published a guide to introduce procurement professionals to the key concepts behind ethical procurement.[28]

CASE STUDY 5 – In practice: Sustainable procurement

Although as a private sector organisation LOCOG was not subject to EU procurement legislation, it adopted fair and sustainable procurement principles and processes. This was delivered through a Procurement Governance Model (PGM) which was administered by the Procurement team, working with key enterprise leads including the Sustainability team. The PGM was also set up as a means to deliver in excess of £75 million savings against budget and had full support from senior management.

A supporting Sustainable Sourcing Code was produced which set out its requirements in detail and applied to all commercial suppliers, sponsors and merchandise licensees. It was not intended to be prescriptive – it instead set out a framework to enable LOCOG to consider the relevant issues and make informed choices by applying a set of core principles throughout. These were:

- Responsible sourcing
- Use of secondary materials
- Minimising embodied impacts
- Healthy materials

Put simply, its approach to sourcing more sustainable products was based on asking the following questions:

1. Where does it come from?
2. Who made it?
3. What is it made of?
4. What is it wrapped in?
5. What would happen to it after the Games?

On occasions when it sourced services involving labour, it used the Ethical Trading Initiative Base Code[29] as the required standard that suppliers were to work towards.

The Sourcing Code also contained a number of core obligations of suppliers, sponsors and licensees including the requirement to integrate it into their management processes, obligations around community benefits, supply of information including LOCOG's right to audit and disclosure of production site locations by suppliers, use of subcontractors and third parties, claims and declarations, and dispute resolution procedures. The Code also included an indicative list of spend categories and how each area of the Code was likely to apply.

Commercial deals of at least £250,000 in value, or which were considered to result in a significant relationship, were decided by a Deal Approval Group. This was chaired by the General Counsel and attended by the Head of Procurement and Head of Sustainability.

A range of sustainability tools and resources were utilised and developed to further support LOCOG and its supply chain in the management of risks and opportunities. Any issues that could not be resolved could be escalated through existing governance mechanisms such as the Deal Approval Group.

Additional information

- LOCOG Sustainable Sourcing Code: **http://learninglegacy.independent.gov.uk/documents/pdfs/sustainability/cp-locog-sustainable-sourcing-code.pdf**

- Sustainable procurement lessons learned paper: **http://learninglegacy.independent.gov.uk/documents/pdfs/sustainability/cs-games-sustainable-procurement.pdf**
- Supply chain grievance mechanism lessons learned paper: **http://learninglegacy.independent.gov.uk/documents/pdfs/sustainability/cs-sustainable-sourcing-code-complaints-mechanism.pdf**
- Stakeholder Oversight Group lessons learned paper: **http://learninglegacy.independent.gov.uk/documents/pdfs/sustainability/cs-establishing-a-stakeholder-oversight-group.pdf**
- Independent review of how compliance with labour standards were managed: **http://learninglegacy.independent.gov.uk/documents/pdfs/sustainability/rs-managing-compliance-with-labour-standards-final.pdf**

Communications

Sustainability is an incredibly complex subject to communicate. It may well be necessary to simplify messages and talk in a language people can relate to and understand. You may also be competing with other business communications 'priorities' both externally and internally – your communications or internal engagement teams may not even see sustainability as a priority at all. Regardless, it is very important that you do attempt to communicate your efforts to your internal and external stakeholders.

There are a number of reasons why you should do this:

- ✓ Raise and maintain awareness of your sustainability programme and promote achievements – maximise opportunities to tell your sustainability story;
- ✓ Build stronger stakeholder relationships and partnerships;
- ✓ Generate positive media coverage; and
- ✓ Receive and respond to enquiries, concerns or other stakeholder feedback including reacting to potential negative media issues.

It is advisable to develop a communications strategy and plan for your organisation that is regularly reviewed and revised. This may sit as part of your sustainability stakeholder engagement strategy or plan or be separate – regardless they should mutually complement each other. Any approach should link closely with the work of other relevant departments and teams (e.g. communications and public affairs, marketing, investor relations and so on). Dissemination of sustainability messages should be both direct and embedded in other communications – and joined up!

Key questions to ask when setting out how you will approach internal and external communications include:

Internal communi-cations	• How does sustainability fit into your wider internal communications plans? • Do you know what sustainability information should be circulated internally, when and to whom? • Are employees informed of agreed external sustainability messages/lines?

	• How do you communicate sustainability information to employees and contractors? • How do you communicate sustainability achievements internally? • How do you encourage feedback from employees and contractors?
External communi-cations	• How does sustainability fit into your wider external communications plans? • Do you know who your external stakeholders are and what information they are interested in and when they would like it? • How do you communicate sustainability information to key stakeholders? • What is your sustainability narrative? How does this fit with your significant (or 'material' issues)? What are your key sustainability messages and lines? • Do you know or have relationships with key sustainability media/journalists? • Who is authorised to speak to mainstream and trade press/media? Have they been appropriately trained? • How do you receive and respond to external enquiries on sustainability matters? Are the right people informed or consulted internally? • Do you have communications lines prepared on key aspects of your programme – e.g. targets or issues where you do not necessarily have a firm policy stance?

- Do you consider sustainability angles to wider communications to ensure joined up messaging – e.g. could a press release announce something that is at complete odds with your sustainability vision?
- Do you have processes in place to respond to potential negative press?

There are a number of mechanisms for communication and range from the low-tech to the high-tech and could be proactive or reactive.

Internally mechanisms may include meeting minutes, newsletters, road-shows, suggestion boxes, email and Intranet, centrally administered screensavers, special engagement campaigns, committees, competitions, and use of gamification techniques.

Mechanisms for external communication may include informal discussion, supplier forums and industry days, tender documentation, focus groups, community events, websites, newsletters, press releases, sustainability reports, marketing campaigns, conferences and seminars, entering awards, media days, use of recognised individuals or celebrities to act as ambassadors or champions of your cause, and of course social media such as blogging, Facebook and Twitter.

Most organisations rightly have very firm stances on who is and who is not authorised to speak to the press and media. This may differ depending on whether this is a mainstream journalist (e.g. BBC, *Daily Telegraph*, etc.) or trade journalist (e.g. *ENDS Report*, Edie, Ethical Corporation, or specialist trade magazine). Consequently, sustainability focused media training may be restricted to only those who are likely and authorised to be interviewed by journalists. This is potentially a missed opportunity though as such training is also useful to any individuals with sustainability responsibilities who may be confronted with an incredibly difficult stakeholder situation (for example, responding to NGO allegations or defending policy positions in a public forum).

Documented information

The final thing to think about at this stage in the process is getting the right balance between having appropriate documentation and other demonstrable actions. Documentation and records are likely to be located in various places and forms (paper, electronic, etc.) around the business.

Two key considerations at this stage are:

1. What if someone completely independent of your organisation came in to review your arrangements - would they be able to determine how sustainability issues are being managed?

2. If individuals responsible for key areas of your management system are suddenly incapacitated (the 'knocked down by a bus' analogy) - would it be clear to someone stepping into their shoes on what needs to be done?

It is therefore very advisable to summarise your management system arrangements in the form of a manual. This should provide an overview of your sustainability strategy and the systems in place to underpin its delivery, for example, how management processes have been influenced to consider sustainability matters. It should also provide signposting to related processes and documentation or indeed set out the arrangements where documentation does not formally exist elsewhere. It is also a good idea to outline your framework conceptually (see Figure 4 for an example of what this might look like).

FIGURE 4. Example conceptual overview of a sustainability management system.

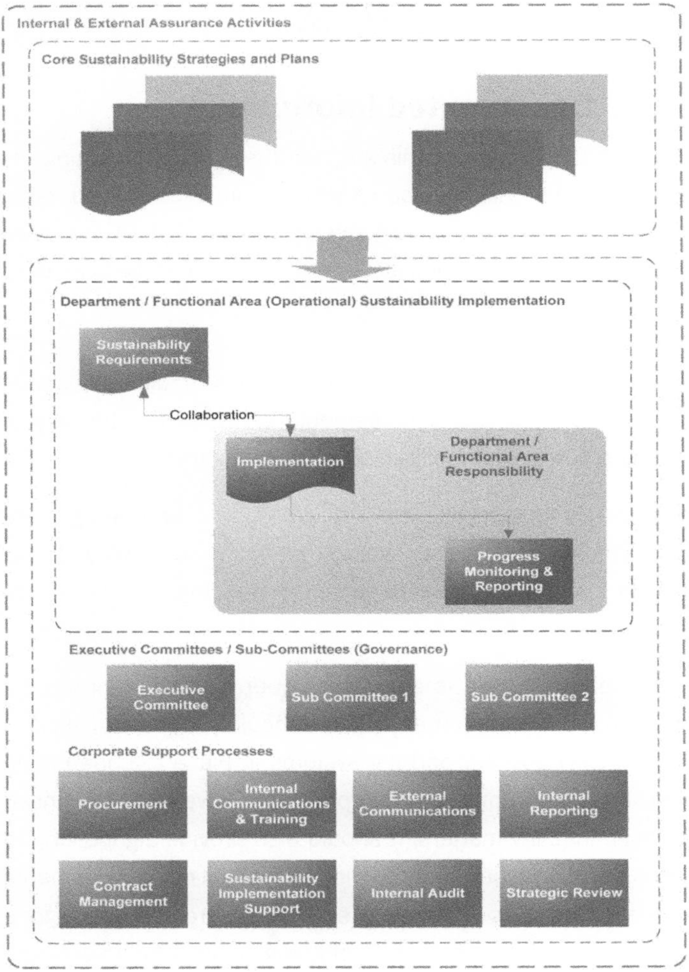

You should also follow your organisation's process for controlling documents so that it is clear to you and others which document is the latest version and where it can be found. If your organisation does not have a formalised system for version control then come up with something that works for you. At the very least an official document should be clearly marked with a date and a version number.

CHAPTER 5

Is Everything up to Scratch?

Orientation: Where you are in the process

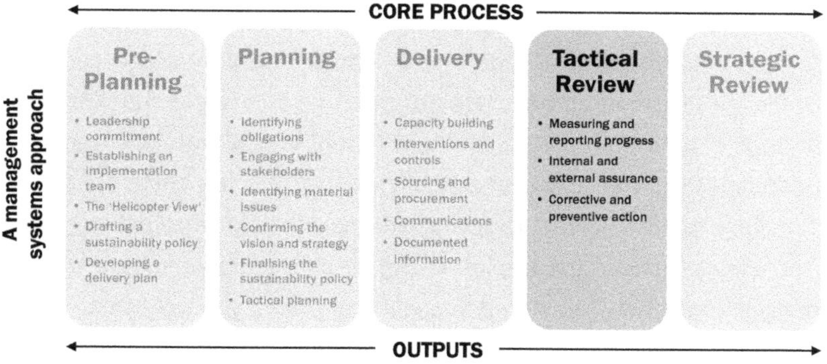

HOPEFULLY, YOUR MANAGEMENT SYSTEMS APPROACH will be helping your organisation to improve its sustainability performance. This section outlines some things to think about when evaluating your arrangements and how they're performing. Ideally, action should be taken to prevent possible problems before they occur or at least correct issues before they get completely out of hand. Think of this stage in the process as more of an ongoing 'tactical' review.

Measuring and reporting progress

You need to think about what arrangements are required to regularly monitor and measure key areas of your organisation that affect delivery of your strategy and associated goals.

Some records will be required in order to effectively track performance, how effective your critical process interventions are and how you are doing in respect to any objectives or targets. That said, identifying what needs to be measured including who, when and how is easier said than done. Data collection is often a very difficult area to get right and many organisations do struggle.

Gathering information and data is a complicated task and a constant challenge. Information and data are often held in numerous places, in a range of different formats, and by different teams that have their own priorities. Data may also not actually exist or are too costly to obtain. Timelines for internal reporting and external reporting may not align. It is also easy to fall into the trap of asking for information and data without really knowing how you intend to use it – or even if you will use it.

Key questions to ask at this stage in respect to data measures and sources are as follows:

- What data are appropriate to the boundaries of your sustainability strategy and other initiatives you intend to participate in?
- What data are relevant to any objectives, milestones and targets you have established?
- What data are required for use in ongoing engagement with stakeholders including top management?

Your review should include consideration of whether you intend, or are required, to report internally or externally and to whom. For instance, do you intend to also report in accordance with Global Reporting Initiative (GRI) requirements or respond to external ratings initiatives such as the Dow Jones Sustainability Index, Business in the Community or the Carbon Disclosure Project? Such requirements may be over and above what your strategy is designed to achieve and may or may not be aligned with your objectives and targets. An earlier DōShort outlines how to measure, manage and account for sustainability (albeit only in the context of GRI).[30] *The Short Guide to Sustainable Investing*[31] is also worth reviewing too.

Reporting should not be underestimated and should be considered alongside developing any sustainability strategy and associated objectives and targets. Knowing what is definitely required versus what is perhaps only a 'nice to have' or not required at all will avoid a lot of wasted time and resources down the line.

Even if you are looking to establish an ambitious objective and it is not clear how you will measure it then at least you have identified this upfront and can be included as part of a forward action programme. This is likely to be a particular challenge when attempting to measure more strategic level goals (see next chapter).

It is advisable to develop a clear plan for your data collection needs which identifies roles and responsibilities, how and when data should be reported, and how data are managed (for instance, do you intend to use spreadsheets or also make use of proprietary sustainability software). Any equipment required for gathering of data (e.g. a sound level meter) should be fit for purpose and calibrated and maintained appropriately. At some point your data collection arrangements may well be internally or externally audited.

Progress can and should of course also be measured objectively. You should ideally be looking to feed into any internal reporting processes that exist within the organisation. This could be internal within the department or team or through wider governance reporting arrangements that exist (e.g. convening top management committees).

Regardless, sustainability performance reports should be prepared on a regular basis (e.g. quarterly) with input from other relevant departments and teams. This should include consideration of:

- Material or significant issues;
- Risks and opportunities;
- Compliance with legislation and other obligations;
- Stakeholder concerns;
- Progress towards any objectives and targets;
- Results of any assurance activities (see below); and
- Lessons learned and any recommended actions.

This process will help with any strategic review that is undertaken (see next chapter) and can be used to input into wider internal and external reporting requirements. Repeating the 'Helicopter View' or 'stock-take' exercise is also advisable to do on a periodic basis to coincide with any strategic review you do.

CASE STUDY 6 – In practice: Data collection and management

Kingfisher plc have committed to managing and improving their impacts across all their Operating Companies and aim to transform the way they operate to become Net Positive in four priority areas by 2050. They currently measure their progress against 50 milestones and targets, which have been established for 2016 and 2020, respectively. These cover their Net Positive priorities (timber, energy, innovation, communities) and three other areas (employees, suppliers and partners, environment).

In some cases specific guidance and tools have been developed to set out how targets are defined and measured. For example, as there is currently no universally accepted definition of 'eco-products' they worked with BioRegional Development Group to develop their own.

With the launch of Net Positive in October 2012 they are in the process of expanding their data collection systems and developing additional impact measures for their 2050 aspirations.

Kingfisher is working with their operating companies to integrate their vision and targets into their businesses. Each operating company has developed a four-year plan for how it will contribute to meeting Net Positive targets and milestones within its businesses. They are also required to complete the following questionnaires via an online portal which are used to monitor their progress:

- Key performance indicator (KPI) questionnaire to monitor data trends. This is completed on an annual basis, with the exception of eco-product data which are collected quarterly; and
- Foundations questionnaire to monitor progress against targets and milestones. This is completed once a year.

At group level there is a dedicated data analyst who oversees the collection and management of Net Positive data.

The CEO of each operating company is responsible for ensuring that appropriate processes and controls are in place to monitor and report progress against Net Positive targets and milestones. They are required to complete an annual self-certification to confirm that submitted performance data are materially accurate and have been subject to an appropriate level of review prior to submission.

Kingfisher also works with internal audit and external assurance providers to review data. For example, they have used BioRegional Development Group to externally review eco-product data and have used Efeca (lead consultants to the UK government's timber procurement policy) to externally review timber data.

They have set out the scope and methodologies used to calculate their data in a detailed document which is available on their website.

Additional information

- Net Positive data collection methodology: **http://files.the-group.net/library/kgf/responsibility/pdfs/cr_27.pdf**

- Foundations Questionnaire scoring guide: **http://files.the-group.net/library/kgf/responsibility/pdfs/cr_27.pdf**

Internal and external assurance

Assurance can take many forms from independent audits of particular areas, independent verification of data, through to internal audit activities sponsored by top management or reviews of supplier performance by contract managers.

If correctly executed assurance should add a lot of value and help you determine whether your system is working and is properly implemented or identify improvement opportunities.

There are likely to be a number of assurance activities taking place within your organisation. You should be looking to dovetail your sustainability requirements into these activities as much as possible, particularly where results are reported to top management such as formal internal audit programmes. This will enable any gaps to be addressed by specific interventions you introduce.

One approach is to prepare an integrated programme to direct which areas of your management system should be looked at using a range of assurance activities and approaches. It is not necessary to look at the entirety of the system as part of one audit but over time all elements should be reviewed. All assurance activities should have clear objectives established. Timing of reviews, frequency of audits, role of the supply chain, roles and responsibilities, and how results will be communicated to top management are all things that need to be considered.

Assurance activities may be classified in a number of ways but here is one suggested approach to consider when preparing your programme:

A. **System audits** – analysis of management system elements classified according to:

    1. Corporate or central arrangements
    2. Localised arrangements

B. **Department, functional or programme audits** – analysis of sustainability elements specific to a department, team or programme (including work streams) classified according to:

    1. Dedicated sustainability audits
    2. Multi-issue audits, which include sustainability matters

C. **Subject audits** – analysis of a specific element of sustainability (e.g. waste management, carbon, etc.)

D. **Direct supplier or contractor audits** – audits of direct suppliers and contractors (these may be carried out internally or by third parties) and are classified according to:

    1. Dedicated sustainability audits (e.g. environmental management and/health and safety management audits of site contractors)
    2. Multi-issue audits, which include sustainability matters

E. **Extended supply chain audits** – audits of production sites used by suppliers and which are deemed to be of significant risk to the reputation of the organisation (these may be carried out internally or by third parties)

F. External assurance reviews such as:

   1. Specialist reviews undertaken by organisations that have an interest in the organisation but are technically independent of it

   2. Reasonable or limited assurance engagements

Individuals undertaking assurance activities should be objective, impartial and competent. This applies to individuals who are internal or external to the organisation.

Processes and controls to manage sustainability issues will help you achieve a level of assurance over key aspects of your programme. Controls can be implemented across different levels of the organisation as illustrated by the three 'lines of defence' approach below. This approach sets out control methods according to the three key levels of the organisation where the risk of non-compliance is mitigated. Each 'line' plays an important role in reducing the risk of error or uncertainty to an acceptable level and results in improved processes and controls (see Figure 5).

This approach means that individuals or teams with sustainability responsibilities have a role to play in supporting assurance activities. Such individuals or teams will have established the operational management measures (first line), and will provide a level of oversight as these measures are implemented (second line). The third and final line of defence in respect to assurance activities though should always be performed by individuals (internal or external) who have not been directly involved in developing processes and controls (the management system). This approach will work for all sizes of organisations. The level of internal and external challenge required will clearly be dependent on the nature and scale of the business.

FIGURE 5. Three 'lines of defence' assurance approach.

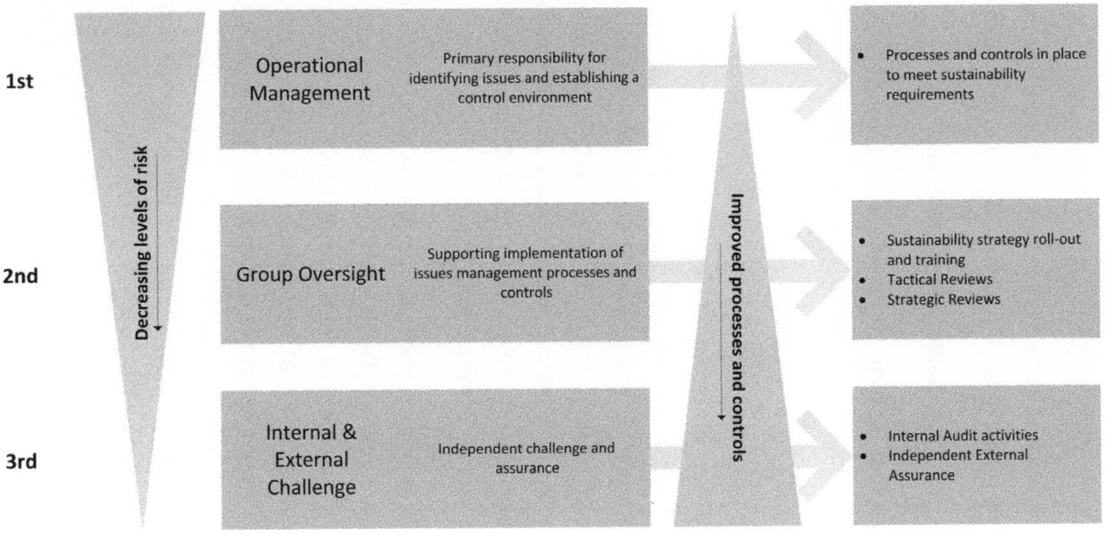

SOURCE: LOCOG.

Corrective and preventive action

By this stage you should find yourself in a position where situations are being bought to your attention that may not quite be as they should be. Things are unlikely to ever be perfect or run as smoothly as you would like. There may be a number of reasons for this and could include (amongst other things):

- Individuals or teams not knowing that they are responsible for doing something - or may know but are not competent for the task at hand;
- A process or part of a process is not being followed - or may be followed but not actually working in practice;
- A breach of policy or the law has occurred or is occurring;
- A previously unforeseen sustainability issue has arisen and there are no arrangements to manage it;
- Suppliers not meeting their contractual requirements; or
- Objectives and targets are not on course to be met

These anomalies can be identified through a variety of means, such as ongoing assurance activities including contractor audits, internal reporting arrangements including your own performance reviews, concerns raised by stakeholders, lessons learned, or indeed by individuals or teams who bring things to your attention directly.

You will need some form of process to address these anomalies and you should be looking to address the root cause. For example, is the issue a one-off or is it an endemic issue within the organisation? You should be seeking to identify why the anomaly has occurred and what should be done to prevent it from reoccurring in the future.

CHAPTER 6

Practice Makes Perfect

Orientation: Where you are in the process

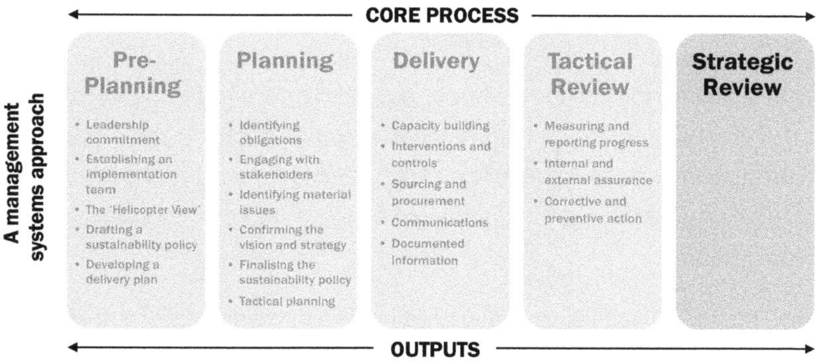

IF SUSTAINABLE DEVELOPMENT is the process by which we move towards improved sustainability over time then your management systems approach should support this goal by also continuously evolving and improving over time.

You need to be in a position to take a step back and determine whether your organisation is on track to deliver its sustainability strategy and associated goals and perhaps, more importantly, is actually improving its sustainability performance.

As sustainability is a cross-cutting theme with significant political, public and corporate aspects, it is important for top management to receive a full briefing in addition to normal internal reporting channels.

A strategic (or management) review is arguably the most important part of the management system and should be undertaken on a periodic basis. Many organisations that adopt management systems standards undertake this type of review on an annual basis (to varying levels of success). In the context of sustainability it is considered that half-yearly is a more appropriate time period for strategic reviews (for most organisations anyway).

Whilst any performance reviews or audits will have determined whether arrangements are being followed (see previous section), the purpose of a strategic review is to determine whether the system meets the needs of your organisation and is actually helping it improve its sustainability performance.

Key inputs will include any sustainability performance reports that have been prepared which consider the results of assurance activities, issues and concerns raised by stakeholders, performance against objectives and targets, issues and risks, incidents and recommendations for improvements. The outcomes of any periodic 'Helicopter View' or 'stock-take' exercises should also be considered.

A summary of key issues and topics of concern and any initial recommendations for improving aspects of the management system should be prepared ahead of time. This should then be presented and discussed with key managers and top management itself. Resulting actions may include decisions on:

- Changes to the *entire* strategy and management systems approach;

- Additional resources required to support delivery;
- Amendments to existing policies, processes or objectives and targets; and
- Additional policies, processes or objectives and targets that may be required

Evaluating strategic performance is an area that many organisations are grappling with at the moment – for example, how can you know for sure you are moving towards improved sustainability? Nobody really seems to have a definitive answer to this yet. There are various approaches and methods that are being advocated or trialled from qualitative approaches (e.g. a maturity matrix approach is recommended in BS 8900 and ISO 20121) to more complicated quantitative approaches (e.g. Natural Capital Accounting[32]). Given the multi-faceted nature of sustainability it is unlikely though that any one measure will deliver success in terms of monitoring and review of overall performance – but watch this space. . .

CHAPTER 7

Conclusion and Final Thoughts

THE INTENTION OF THIS DŌSHORT has been to introduce you to management systems thinking and concepts to help you put in place a framework, by tapping into or supplementing existing arrangements as much as possible, to bridge the gap between your strategy and what you want to achieve – from a non-standards viewpoint.

A lot of things are likely to be in place already. Adopting a management systems approach will help you in being more formalised and systematic in how and when you do things. It will help people understand what sustainability means and more importantly how it applies to their organisation or role. It will strengthen the link between strategy and action and provide the framework for various things to happen.

Hopefully, most of what has been covered in previous chapters has highlighted a number of things your organisation is already doing or with a few simple tweaks could do straight away. The process should work for all types of organisations however big or small. In fact, small- and medium-sized businesses may even find it easier to adopt a management systems approach to improve their sustainability performance than larger organisations (contrary to popular belief!).

It is incredibly important that you take time to understand the prevailing culture of the organisation. A well thought-out and documented management system is totally useless if no one follows it.

Ultimately the intention has been to help you identify what could be done to embed a more sustainable approach more securely throughout your organisation. There is no right or wrong answer to how this should be done. Any step you take to embed sustainability will make a difference no matter how small the action or initiative.

Some final thoughts. . .

How serious a business is with embedding sustainability into their organisation is largely down to the whim and commitment of its top management. If key executives and proponents move on or have a change of heart then this will put everything you have strived to achieve at risk – no matter how solid your management system foundations are or successful your achievements.

One option is to explore whether your organisation's constitution can be amended to include a commitment to operate in a sustainable manner. For many organisations this would involve formally amending the Memorandum and Articles of Association with Companies House. That is not to say that any future commitment to sustainability is risk-free but it does mean that it would be more difficult for it to be completely dropped from the business agenda as a result in a change in leadership.

There are a couple of known examples where this has been happened and has been very successful. For example, the Joint Venture Agreement which established LOCOG as the private body responsible for planning and staging the London 2012 Games introduced the requirement for it to have 'due regard to the principles of Sustainable Development'.[33] The London Olympic Games and Paralympic Games Act 2006 which established the Olympic Delivery Authority included similar provisions.[34]

And finally most organisations are grappling with the same issues and challenges. Sharing lessons learned on the management approaches that have been taken or attempted to improve sustainability performance including what worked *and* what didn't (which is equally important) would be of considerable benefit. This could be included as part of sustainability reporting, although is rarely done, or as separate case studies and again seldom is. As your own knowledge and understanding advances there will be learnings (good and bad) and you may well identify new ideas and ways of working. Sharing this information should lead to a better outcome for everyone.

In establishing your objectives and targets you should ideally be looking to make a commitment to share what you have learned to help advance the practices that improve sustainability not only within your own organisation but wider industry too.

Notes

1. BS 8900-1:2013, Managing sustainable development of organizations - Part 1: Guide, BSI, 2013.
2. BS 8900-2:2013, Managing sustainable development of organizations - Part 2: Framework for assessment against BS 8900-1 - Specification, BSI, 2013.
3. BS ISO 20121:2012, Event sustainability management systems - Requirements with guidance for use, BSI, 2012.
4. BS ISO 26000:2010, Guidance on social responsibility, BSI, 2010.
5. **http://www.projectsigma.co.uk**
6. **https://www.globalreporting.org/reporting/g4**
7. BS EN ISO 9001:2008, Quality management systems - Requirements, BSI, 2008.
8. BS EN ISO 14001:2004, Environmental management systems - Requirements with guidance for use, BSI, 2004.
9. **http://www.iso.org/iso/home/news_index/news_archive/news.htm?refid=Ref1547**
10. Henriques, Adrian, 2012. *Making the Most of Standards - The Sustainability Professional's Guide* (Oxford: Dō Sustainability).
11. **https://www.deming.org/theman/theories/pdsacycle**
12. McKay, Alexandra, 2013. *Strategic Sustainability - Why it Matters to Your Business and How to Make It Happen* (Oxford: Dō Sustainability).
13. **http://www.ends.co.uk/47/**

NOTES

14. Cumming, Phil and Pelham, Fiona, 2011. *Making Events More Sustainable – A Guide to BS 8901* (London: BSI).

15. Mendelow, Aubrey, 1981. *Environmental scanning: The impact of the stakeholder concept. In Proceedings from the second international conference on information systems* (Cambridge, MA)

16. AA1000 Stakeholder Engagement Standard AA1000SES, AccountAbility, 2011

17. **http://www.projectsigma.co.uk/Toolkit/SustainabilityIssuesGuide.pdf**

18. **http://www.unglobalcompact.org/abouttheGC/TheTenPrinciples/index.html**

19. **http://www.oneplanetliving.net/what-is-one-planet-living/the-ten-principles/**

20. **http://www.kingfisher.co.uk/netpositive/files/downloads/kingfisher_netpos_brochure.pdf**

21. **http://planareport.marksandspencer.com/docs/33722_M&S_PlanA.pdf**

22. **http://www.ikea.com/ms/en_GB/pdf/people_planet_positive/People_planet_positive.pdf**

23. **http://www.ribaplanofwork.com**

24. **http://learninglegacy.independent.gov.uk/documents/pdfs/procurement-and-supply-chain-management/01-concrete-pscm.pdf**

25. **http://www.bis.gov.uk/assets/BISCore/corporate/MigratedD/publications/C/cs02_hmps.pdf**

26. **http://www.j-sainsbury.co.uk/media/373272/sainsbury_s_20_by_20_sustainability_plan.pdf**

27. BS 8903:2010, Principles and framework for procuring sustainably – Guide, BSI, 2010.

28. **http://www.cips.org/Documents/About%20CIPS/CIPS_Ethics_Guide_WEB.pdf**

29. **http://www.ethicaltrade.org/eti-base-code**

30. Musikanski, Laura, 2012. *How to Account for Sustainability: A Simple Guide to Measuring and Managing* (Oxford: Dō Sustainability).

31. Krosinsky, Cary, 2013. *The Short Guide to Sustainable Investing* (Oxford: Dō Sustainability).

32. **http://www.kpmg.com/UK/en/IssuesAndInsights/ArticlesPublications/Documents/PDF/Tax/natural-capital.pdf**

33. **http://learninglegacy.independent.gov.uk/documents/pdfs/sustainability/cs-games-sustainability-management-system.pdf**

34. **http://www.legislation.gov.uk/ukpga/2006/12/crossheading/the-olympic-delivery-authority**

For Product Safety Concerns and Information please contact our EU representative GPSR@taylorandfrancis.com
Taylor & Francis Verlag GmbH, Kaufingerstraße 24, 80331 München, Germany

www.ingramcontent.com/pod-product-compliance
Ingram Content Group UK Ltd.
Pitfield, Milton Keynes, MK11 3LW, UK
UKHW040928180425
457613UK00011B/300

* 9 7 8 1 9 0 9 2 9 3 8 1 6 *